Our Favorite
Melts & Wraps Recipes

Copyright 2010, Gooseberry Patch
Second Printing, February, 2011

There's so much to choose from when serving a sandwich supper! Whole-wheat bread, Hawaiian sweet bread, pumpernickel and hearty country white bread all make delicious sandwiches.

Hoagie Sandwich Bake

Makes 6 servings

2 8-oz. tubes refrigerated
   crescent rolls, divided
1/3 lb. sliced salami
1/3 lb. sliced pepperoni
1/3 lb. sliced deli ham

1/3 lb. sliced Swiss cheese
1/3 lb. sliced provolone cheese
4 eggs, beaten and divided
grated Parmesan cheese to taste

Flatten one tube crescent rolls and press into a greased 13"x9" baking pan. Layer salami, pepperoni and ham over top of rolls. Top with Swiss and provolone cheeses. Brush half of beaten egg evenly over cheeses; cover with remaining rolls. Brush remaining egg over crescent rolls; sprinkle with Parmesan cheese. Bake, uncovered, at 350 degrees for 25 minutes. Cover with aluminum foil; bake for an additional 20 minutes. Slice into squares.

Get out Grandma's cast-iron skillet for the tastiest, toastiest hot sandwiches. Cast iron provides even heat distribution for speedy cooking and crisp golden crusts.

Hometown Diner Patty Melts *Makes 4 sandwiches*

1 onion, thinly sliced
2 to 3 T. butter, softened and divided
1 lb. lean ground beef, formed into 4 thin patties

seasoned salt and pepper to taste
8 slices rye bread
8 slices Swiss cheese

In a skillet over medium heat, cook onion in one tablespoon butter about 10 minutes, until caramelized and golden. On a griddle over medium heat, brown beef patties about 6 minutes per side, or until no longer pink in center. Season beef patties with salt and pepper to taste; set aside. Wipe griddle clean with a paper towel. Spread remaining butter over one side of each bread slice; place 4 slices butter-side down on hot griddle. Top each bread slice with a cheese slice, a beef patty, 1/4 of onion, another cheese slice and another bread slice, butter-side up. Cook sandwiches over medium-low heat until golden on both sides and cheese is melted.

Turn leftover bits & pieces of cheese from the fridge into
a scrumptious sandwich topping. Just shred cheese and
stir in enough mayo to make a spreadable consistency.
Serve on crusty bread...yum!

Grilled Bacon-Tomato Sandwiches   *Serves 4*

8 slices bacon, crisply cooked
1 tomato, sliced
4 slices Cheddar or American
   cheese

8 slices wheat bread, divided
1 to 2 T. butter, softened

Layer bacon, tomato and cheese on 4 slices bread; top with remaining bread. Spread outside of sandwiches with butter. Place sandwiches in a non-stick skillet over medium-low heat. Cook for 4 to 6 minutes, or until golden on both sides.

White paper coffee filters are super for serving up sandwiches
and wraps...no spills, no mess and easy for little hands to hold.
Afterwards, just toss them away.

Grilled Veggie Sandwich

Makes 8 servings

1/4 c. balsamic vinegar
2 T. olive oil
2 t. molasses
1 T. fresh basil, chopped
1-1/2 t. fresh thyme, chopped
1/4 t. salt
1/4 t. pepper
3 zucchini, thinly sliced

1 yellow pepper, sliced
2 red peppers, sliced
1 onion, sliced
16-oz. loaf French bread, halved
3/4 c. crumbled feta cheese
2 T. mayonnaise
1/4 c. fresh Parmesan cheese, grated

Whisk together vinegar, oil, molasses, herbs, salt and pepper. Place vegetables in a plastic zipping bag. Add vinegar mixture; refrigerate for 2 hours, turning bag occasionally. Remove vegetables from bag and set aside, reserving marinade. Brush 3 to 4 tablespoons reserved marinade over cut sides of bread. Coat a grill with non-stick vegetable spray. Grill vegetables for 5 minutes, basting occasionally with remaining marinade; turn and grill an additional 2 minutes, until tender. Grill bread, cut-side down, for 3 minutes, until toasted. Blend feta cheese and mayonnaise; spread over bread. Layer bottom half of bread with vegetables, Parmesan cheese and top half of bread. Slice into 8 sections.

Pack a bottle of frozen lemonade or iced tea with lunch in the morning to keep everything cool. When lunchtime rolls around, enjoy a crisp sandwich wrap and a frosty drink too!

Sam's Terrific Turkey Tortillas   *Makes 10 servings*

10 10-inch flour tortillas
10 slices cooked turkey, sliced
   into thin strips
1 avocado, pitted, peeled and
   sliced

1/2 c. sour cream
1/2 c. shredded Cheddar cheese

Heat flour tortillas in a large skillet over medium heat until slightly
browned. Divide turkey strips, avocado, sour cream and cheese
among the warmed tortillas. Fold in half and serve.

Sandwiches are a tasty solution when family members
will be dining at different times. Fix sandwiches ahead of time,
wrap individually and refrigerate. Pop them into a toaster oven
or under a broiler to heat...fresh, full of flavor
and ready whenever you are!

Apple & Turkey Sandwiches

Serves 4

2 T. jellied cranberry sauce
2 T. mayonnaise
8 slices sourdough bread
1 lb. deli turkey, thinly sliced

1 Granny Smith apple, cored,
  peeled and thinly sliced
1 c. shredded Cheddar cheese

Mix together cranberry sauce and mayonnaise; spread evenly over bread slices. Arrange bread on an ungreased baking sheet. Divide turkey evenly among bread. Top turkey with apple slices; sprinkle with cheese. Broil until cheese is melted and golden.

Leftover grilled chicken makes the best chicken wraps the next day! Simply slice or shred chicken, fill tortillas and serve with salsa and guacamole.

Chicken Florentine Quesadillas

Serves 8 to 10

4 10-inch flour tortillas
8-oz. pkg. frozen spinach-
  artichoke dip, thawed
2 6-oz. pkgs. grilled chicken
  breast strips
1 c. shredded Mexican-blend
  cheese

1/2 red onion, thinly sliced
1/2 c. black olives, sliced
2 roma tomatoes, thinly sliced
1 green pepper, thinly sliced
Optional: sour cream, shredded
  lettuce

Warm tortillas on a griddle. Spread 2 tortillas with dip. Top with chicken strips, cheese and sliced vegetables. Add remaining tortillas; place on a lightly oiled griddle over medium-high heat. Cook for 3 to 5 minutes, until heated through and cheese is melted, using a spatula to carefully turn over. Quesadillas may also be placed on a baking sheet and baked at 375 degrees for about 10 minutes. Using a pizza cutter, cut each quesadilla into 4 to 8 wedges. Garnish with sour cream and shredded lettuce, if desired.

Spice up your favorite ranch salad dressing! To one cup of dressing, whisk in 1/4 teaspoon chili powder and 1/2 teaspoon ground cumin. Let stand 5 minutes for flavors to blend.

Chicken Ranch Quesadillas

Serves 4

1/2 c. ranch dip
8 8-inch flour tortillas
1 c. shredded Cheddar cheese
1 c. shredded Monterey Jack
    cheese

10-oz. can chicken, drained
1/3 c. bacon bits
Optional: salsa

Spread 2 tablespoons dip on 4 tortillas. Sprinkle each with 1/4 of Cheddar cheese, Monterey Jack cheese, chicken and bacon bits. Top each with remaining tortillas. Cook each tortilla in a lightly greased non-stick skillet until lightly golden; turn and cook until cheese is melted. Let stand for 2 minutes; slice into wedges. Serve with salsa, if desired.

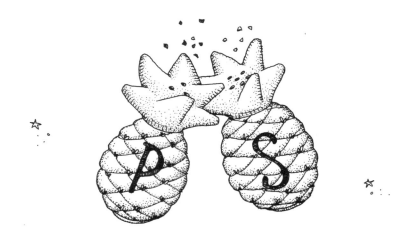

Get out the tiki torches and grass skirts when serving Hula Ham Wraps! Play Hawaiian music, make paper flower leis and make it a family dinner to remember.

Hula Ham Wraps

3/4 lb. deli ham, sliced into
   strips
20-oz. can pineapple tidbits,
   drained
2 carrots, peeled and shredded
1 head Napa cabbage, shredded

1 c. sour cream
1/4 c. white wine vinegar
1 t. salt
1/4 t. pepper
Optional: 1 t. caraway seed
12 10-inch flour tortillas

Combine ham, pineapple, carrots and cabbage in a large bowl; set
aside. In a separate bowl, whisk together sour cream, vinegar, salt,
pepper and caraway seed, if using. Spoon over ham mixture; toss.
Divide among tortillas and roll into wraps.

To crisp tortillas for filling, place a few teaspoons of oil
in a skillet and fry tortillas, one at a time, for a few seconds
until crisp. So simple!

Garden Quesadillas

Makes 6 servings

8-oz. pkg. sliced mushrooms
1 zucchini, sliced
1/2 c. green onions, sliced
14-oz. can corn, drained
1 tomato, chopped
1/2 t. dried cilantro

1/4 t. pepper
6 8-inch flour tortillas
1 c. shredded Mexican-blend
   cheese
Garnish: salsa, sour cream

In a skillet sprayed with non-stick vegetable spray, sauté mushrooms,
zucchini and green onions over medium heat until tender. Stir in corn,
tomato, cilantro and pepper; heat through. Spoon mixture onto half of
each tortilla; sprinkle with cheese and fold over. Lightly spray tops of
tortillas with non-stick vegetable spray; arrange on an ungreased
baking sheet. Bake at 400 degrees for 10 to 12 minutes, until golden.
Cut into wedges; garnish with salsa and sour cream.

Softened cream cheese is perfect for piping into
cherry tomatoes, pea pods or onto celery sticks...terrific
served alongside sandwiches of all kinds.

Pita Tuna Melts

2 6-inch pita rounds
6-oz. can tuna, drained
1 T. mayonnaise
1 T. dill pickle relish
1/4 t. dill weed

1/8 t. salt
1/2 tomato, cut into thin
 wedges
1/2 c. shredded Cheddar cheese

Arrange pitas on an ungreased baking sheet. Bake at 400 degrees for 5 minutes, or until lightly toasted. Mix together tuna, mayonnaise, relish, dill weed and salt in a small bowl; spread onto pitas. Arrange tomato wedges on top; sprinkle with cheese. Bake for an additional 5 minutes, until cheese melts.

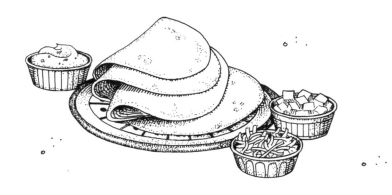

Roasted Corn Salsa...yum! Grill 3 ears corn and slice off kernels. Toss with two diced tomatoes, a diced red pepper, a diced red onion, a seeded, minced jalapeño, 1/2 bunch chopped fresh cilantro, 1/2 cup red wine vinegar and 2 tablespoons olive oil. Chill.

Grilled Salmon Quesadillas

Makes 4 servings

1/2 lb. salmon fillet, 3/4-inch thick
8 6-inch flour tortillas
1 c. shredded Monterey Jack cheese

1/2 c. shredded Cheddar cheese
1/4 to 1/2 c. butter
Garnish: Roasted Corn Salsa (opposite page)

Place salmon on a grill over medium-high heat. Cover and grill for 5 minutes on each side, until fish flakes easily. Let cool; flake with a fork. Divide salmon and cheeses among 4 tortillas; top with remaining tortillas. Melt butter in a large non-stick skillet over high heat. Cook quesadillas, one at a time, until lightly golden and cheese is melted. Cut each into quarters; serve with Roasted Corn Salsa.

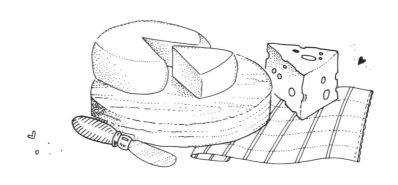

Many's the long night I've dreamed of cheese...toasted, mostly.

-Robert Louis Stevenson

Cheesy Tuna Triangles

Makes 8

1 T. oil
1 c. apple, cored and chopped
3 T. onion, chopped
7-oz. can tuna, drained
1/4 c. chopped walnuts
1/4 c. mayonnaise
2 t. lemon juice

1/8 t. salt
1/8 t. pepper
4 slices raisin bread, toasted
   and halved diagonally
4 slices sharp Cheddar cheese,
   halved diagonally

Heat oil in a skillet over medium heat; add apple and onion. Cook, stirring occasionally, about 5 minutes until tender. Remove from heat; transfer to a bowl. Stir in tuna, walnuts, mayonnaise, lemon juice, salt and pepper. Place toast slices on an ungreased baking sheet. Top with tuna mixture and a slice of cheese. Broil 4 to 5 inches from heat for 3 to 4 minutes, or until cheese begins to melt.

Easy lunchbox dippers! Wrap apple slices and send along a cup of peanut butter for dipping. Try packing salsa, cream cheese or creamy salad dressing for dipping celery or carrot sticks.

Lunchbox Pita Pockets

Makes 6 servings

1-1/2 c. yogurt
1-1/2 c. cucumber, diced
1-1/2 t. fresh parsley, chopped
1/2 t. garlic powder
1/8 t. salt
1/2 t. sugar
hot pepper sauce to taste

6 sausage patties
3 pita rounds, sliced in half
1 tomato, sliced
1 green pepper, sliced
1/2 head lettuce, torn
1/2 sweet onion, thinly sliced
1 c. shredded Cheddar cheese

Combine yogurt, cucumber and seasonings in a medium-size bowl; mix well. Cover and refrigerate until ready to use. Prepare sausage patties according to package directions. Gently open up pita pockets; fill equally with a sausage patty, vegetables and cheese. Spoon in cucumber sauce; wrap tightly in wax paper and refrigerate until serving.

Try packing pita bread, flatbread or tortillas for camping,
instead of regular loaf bread. They won't crush when
packed...tasty warmed up on a griddle over the fire too.

Fireside Reubens

Makes 4 sandwiches

8 slices pumpernickel bread	3/4 lb. deli corned beef, sliced
1 c. Thousand Island salad dressing	1/2 lb. Swiss cheese, sliced
	1 c. sauerkraut, drained

Cut 4 large squares of aluminum foil. Place 2 slices of bread, side-by-side, on each piece of foil. Spread bread slices with salad dressing. Evenly divide corned beef, cheese and sauerkraut among bread. Top with a second slice of bread to make a sandwich. Wrap aluminum foil around sandwiches; seal well. Place packets on a preheated grill over low heat. Cook, turning every 10 minutes, until bread is lightly toasted and cheese is melted, about 30 minutes.

Gather everyone for a fireside meal...so cozy on a chilly day!
Use pie irons to make pocket pies...you can even roast
foil-wrapped potatoes in the coals. Make s'mores
for a sweet ending.

Pie-Iron Tomato Sandwiches

Serves 6 to 8

12 to 16 slices bread
1/4 c. butter, softened
4 tomatoes, sliced

2 onions, sliced
salt and pepper to taste

Spread bread slices with butter; top half of the slices with tomatoes and onions. Sprinkle with salt and pepper to taste. Top with remaining bread slices, butter-side up. Place sandwiches in an ungreased pie iron and place on coals until toasted, about 4 to 6 minutes.

If time's short, pick up a bag of tossed salad greens from the local grocery and toss on a variety of toppings to make it special. Try crumbled blue or feta cheese, freshly chopped herbs, sweetened dried cranberries, apple slices and walnuts...yum!

Chicken & Veggie Wraps

Serves 4

8-oz. container garden
 vegetable cream cheese,
 softened
3 T. mayonnaise
4 8-inch flour tortillas
2 c. romaine lettuce, shredded

1/4 c. sun-dried tomatoes,
 thinly sliced
8 slices provolone cheese
4 green onions, sliced
2 c. cooked chicken, diced

Whisk together cream cheese and mayonnaise until well blended;
spread over tortillas. Top with lettuce, tomatoes, cheese, onions and
chicken. Roll up tightly; cut in half to serve.

Invite family & friends to share a simple supper, then
set out a variety of games and puzzles. Pull out your childhood
favorites...sure to spark memories and laughter!

Cheesy Chicken Pockets

Makes 4 servings

2 T. butter
2 T. all-purpose flour
1/3 c. milk
1/2 c. chicken broth
1/2 t. nutmeg
1/4 t. salt
1/4 t. pepper
1-1/2 c. shredded Cheddar
    cheese

3 slices bacon, crisply cooked
    and crumbled
2 boneless, skinless chicken
    breasts, cooked and
    chopped
2 sheets frozen puff pastry,
    thawed and quartered

In a saucepan, melt butter over medium-high heat. Stir in flour and mix well. Add milk, broth and seasonings; mix well. Bring to a boil over medium heat; cook until thick enough to coat the back of a spoon. Stir in cheese and bacon; mix until cheese melts. Stir in chicken. Arrange 4 quartered pieces of puff pastry on a greased baking sheet. Spoon 1/4 of chicken mixture onto each piece. Top with remaining puff pastry; press edges down with a fork to seal. Bake at 400 degrees for 15 to 18 minutes. Cool for 5 minutes before serving.

Keep browned ground beef on hand for easy meal prep.
Crumble several pounds of beef onto a baking pan and
bake at 350 degrees until browned through, stirring often.
Drain well and pack recipe portions in freezer bags.

Hearty Stew Pockets

Makes 8 servings

2 c. buttermilk biscuit
    baking mix
2 c. all-purpose flour
3/4 t. salt
1 c. margarine, softened
water
1-1/2 lbs. ground beef,
    browned and drained

1 onion, chopped
2 carrots, peeled and coarsely
    grated
6 potatoes, peeled and diced
salt and pepper to taste
8 t. butter, divided

Combine biscuit mix, flour, salt and margarine together; add enough water to make a dough that can be rolled out. Divide into 8 balls; roll each out into a 6-inch circle. In a bowl, combine ground beef, onion, carrot, potatoes, salt and pepper; spoon into center of each circle of dough. Dot one teaspoon butter on top of filling; fold over dough and pinch to seal edges. Place on an ungreased baking sheet. Bake at 350 degrees for one hour.

Pick up a stack of retro-style plastic burger baskets.
Lined with crisp paper napkins, they're such fun for serving
sandwiches with a side of potato chips or crisp veggies.

Ham Biscuits

Makes 24 servings

24 brown & serve dinner
   rolls, halved horizontally
16 slices Swiss cheese
12 slices deli ham
1/2 c. butter, melted

1 T. mustard
1 T. onion powder
1 T. Worcestershire sauce
1 T. poppy seed

On the bottom layer of rolls, layer half the cheese, all the ham and
remaining cheese. Add top layer of rolls and arrange on an ungreased
baking sheet. Combine butter and remaining ingredients; brush on
tops of rolls. Bake at 350 degrees for 15 to 20 minutes, or until
cheese is melted and tops are golden.

Grill juicy ripe peaches for an easy dessert. Brush peach halves with melted butter and place cut-side down on a hot grill. Cook for several minutes, until tender and golden. Drizzle with honey or raspberry preserves...scrumptious!

Grilled Ham Panini

Makes one sandwich

2 slices sourdough bread
1 T. mayonnaise
3 to 6 slices deli smoked ham

2 slices tomato
1 slice American cheese

Spread both slices of bread with mayonnaise on one side. Top one slice with ham, tomato, cheese and remaining bread slice. Spray a griddle or skillet with non-stick vegetable spray. Place sandwich on griddle; set a bacon press or other weight on top. Cook sandwich over medium heat for about 5 minutes, or until toasted and lightly golden on both sides.

Let your countertop meat grill do double duty...it's terrific for
grilling thick sandwiches to perfection.

Philly Turkey Panini

8 slices rye or pumpernickel
   bread
2 T. butter, softened

1/2 lb. deli turkey, thinly sliced
4 slices mozzarella cheese

Spread one side of each bread slice with butter. Arrange 4 bread slices, butter-side down, in a skillet; top with turkey and cheese. Top with remaining bread slices, butter-side up. Cover and cook over medium heat for 4 to 5 minutes, turning once, until bread is crisp and cheese is melted.

Reduced-fat cheese can become tough when exposed to heat.
For best results in hot sandwiches, grill or bake the rest of the
sandwich first, then add shredded reduced-fat cheese.
The heated ingredients will allow the cheese to melt.

Quick Corned Beef Supreme

Serves 5

5 slices rye bread
1/4 to 1/2 c. Thousand Island
    salad dressing

1-1/4 c. creamy coleslaw
1 lb. sliced deli corned beef
1 lb. sliced Swiss cheese

Place bread on a microwave-safe plate; spread each with one to
2 tablespoons dressing. Top each with 1/4 cup coleslaw, 3 to 4 slices
corned beef and 2 slices Swiss cheese. Microwave on high setting for
one minute. Continue to microwave for an additional minute, or until
cheese melts and corned beef curls.

Good china and candles aren't just for the holidays or special celebrations...use them to brighten everyday meals!

Monte Cristos

Makes 4 servings

1/2 c. butter, divided
8 thin slices bread, crusts
  removed
4 large thin slices ham
4 slices sweet onion

8-oz. pkg. shredded Cheddar
  cheese
4 eggs, beaten
salt and pepper to taste

On a large griddle, melt half the butter; fry 4 slices of bread on one side until golden. Remove from griddle and place slices uncooked sides down. Place a slice of ham, a slice of onion and 1/2 cup cheese on each piece of bread. Place the other slice of bread on top of each stack, with the cooked side down. Whisk eggs with a little salt and pepper; coat outsides of sandwiches with eggs. Melt remaining butter on the griddle; fry sandwiches on each side until golden. Slice each in half diagonally; serve immediately.

National Sandwich Day is November 3rd...celebrate and
serve up a favorite sandwich!

Kentucky Hot Brown

2 T. butter
2 T. all-purpose flour
salt and cayenne pepper to taste
1/4 t. curry powder
1 c. milk
3/4 c. shredded American
 cheese, divided

3/4 c. shredded sharp Cheddar
 cheese, divided
4 slices bread, toasted
4 slices deli roast turkey
8 slices bacon, partially cooked

Melt butter in a saucepan over medium heat; whisk in flour, salt, cayenne pepper and curry. Stir until bubbly. Add milk; cook until thickened. Stir in 1/4 cup American cheese and 1/4 cup Cheddar cheese. Cook until cheese melts; set aside. Place one piece of toast on each of 4 oven-safe plates; place one slice of turkey on top of each. Cover each with cheese sauce; top with remaining cheeses and bacon. Place plates under broiler; broil until bacon is fully cooked.

These yummy pizza rolls are terrific as a party snack too. Just slice into one-inch wide pieces and fasten with wooden picks.

Judy's Pizza Rolls

Serves 8

1 lb. ground beef
1 onion, chopped
1 clove garlic, minced
8-oz. can pizza sauce

dried oregano and basil to taste
2/3 c. mozzarella cheese, diced
8 hot dog buns, split

Sauté ground beef, onion and garlic in a skillet over medium heat; drain. Add pizza sauce, oregano and basil; lower heat and simmer for 30 minutes. Let cool slightly; stir in cheese. Fill buns with beef mixture; wrap individually in aluminum foil. Place on a baking sheet and bake at 425 degrees for 20 minutes.

If busy kids can't get home for dinner, take it to them.
Pack a tailgating basket and enjoy picnicking with them at the
ballpark. Be sure to pack extra for hungry team members.

Pepperoni Calzones

Makes 4

12 frozen rolls, thawed
8-oz. pkg. pepperoni slices
1 c. shredded mozzarella cheese
1 t. Italian seasoning

Optional: sliced mushrooms,
   black olives, green pepper
15-oz. can pizza sauce, warmed

Press 3 rolls together; roll out on a floured surface into a 12-inch circle. Repeat with remaining rolls to make 3 more circles. Combine pepperoni, cheese, seasoning and optional ingredients, as desired. Spoon mixture onto 1/2 of each circle. Fold dough over; pinch edges together to seal well. Arrange on greased baking sheets. Bake at 350 degrees for 20 to 25 minutes, or until golden. Serve with warmed pizza sauce for dipping.

For an elegant yet quick last-minute appetizer, toss a drained jar of Italian antipasto mix with bite-size cubes of mozzarella or provolone cheese.

Deli Stromboli

2 10-oz. tubes refrigerated
   pizza crust
1/2 lb. sliced baked ham,
   divided
1/4 lb. sliced hard salami
1/4 lb. sliced pepperoni

1/4 lb. sliced mozzarella cheese
1/4 lb. sliced provolone cheese
1/4 lb. sliced American cheese
1 c. sliced mushrooms
1/3 c. hot pepper rings
1 onion, sliced

Roll crusts out on a lightly greased baking sheet to completely cover the bottom. Layer 1/4 pound meat, a cheese and then a vegetable; continue for 3 layers, ending with a layer of remaining ham. Fold dough back over top, envelope-style; pinch edges closed, making sure all ingredients are tucked inside. Bake at 425 degrees until golden, about 17 to 25 minutes; let stand 5 to 10 minutes before slicing.

Grilled cheese and tomato soup...is there anything more
comforting? For delicious soup in a jiffy, heat together
a can of condensed tomato soup and a can of diced tomatoes
until hot. Stir in a little cream...yum!

Herbed Cheese Focaccia

Serves 12 to 14

13.8-oz. tube refrigerated pizza
    crust
1 onion, finely chopped
2 cloves garlic, minced
2 T. olive oil

1 t. dried basil
1 t. dried oregano
1/2 t. dried rosemary
1 c. shredded mozzarella cheese

Unroll dough on a greased baking sheet. Press with fingers to form
indentations; set aside. Sauté onion and garlic in oil in a skillet;
remove from heat. Stir in herbs; spread mixture evenly over dough.
Sprinkle with cheese. Bake at 400 degrees for 10 to 15 minutes,
until golden. Slice into squares.

More fun fillings for grilled cheese sandwiches!
Sprinkle with Parmesan cheese, Italian or Cajun seasoning,
chives or even a tiny spoonful of salsa... just grill as usual.

Grilled Gouda Sandwiches

Makes 4 sandwiches

8 slices country-style bread
1 clove garlic, halved
4 t. Dijon mustard
1/2 lb. sliced Gouda cheese

2 T. butter, melted
1/8 t. cayenne pepper
1/8 t. pepper

Rub one side of each slice of bread with garlic. Place 4 bread slices garlic-side down; top each bread slice with one teaspoon mustard and 2 slices Gouda. Place remaining bread slices, garlic-side up, on sandwich bottoms. Combine butter, cayenne pepper and pepper in a small bowl; brush mixture over each side of sandwiches. Cook sandwiches in an oven-proof skillet over medium-high heat for about 2 minutes on each side, until golden. Place skillet in oven and bake at 400 degrees for about 5 minutes, until cheese is melted. Slice sandwiches diagonally.

Delight finicky eaters with jigsaw puzzle sandwiches.
Press a cookie cutter straight down in the center of a sandwich,
then slice the outer part of sandwich into 3 or 4 pieces.
It works great with grilled cheese!

Special Grilled Cheese Sandwich

Makes 4

3-oz. pkg. cream cheese,
   softened
1/2 to 3/4 c. mayonnaise
8-oz. pkg. shredded Colby-Jack
   cheese

3/4 t. garlic powder
1/4 t. salt
8 slices French bread
2 T. butter, softened

Combine all ingredients except bread and butter; blend until smooth.
Spread mixture on 4 slices of bread; top with remaining bread. Spread
butter on outside of sandwiches. Place sandwiches in a large skillet
over medium heat. Grill until golden, about 4 minutes per side.

Good bread is the most fundamentally satisfying of all foods.

-James Beard

Suzanne's Tomato Melt

Makes one serving

1/4 c. shredded Cheddar cheese
1 onion bagel or English muffin,
    split

2 tomato slices
1 T. shredded Parmesan cheese

Sprinkle half the Cheddar cheese over each bagel or English muffin half. Top with a tomato slice. Sprinkle half the Parmesan cheese over each tomato. Broil about 6 inches from heat for 4 to 5 minutes, or until cheese is bubbly.

Onions are delicious in sandwiches but can have a bit of a bite. For a milder flavor, cover sliced onion with cold water and a splash of vinegar for half an hour before using. Drain well and pat dry.

Carol's Veggie Panini

Makes 4 servings

2 T. balsamic vinegar
1 T. olive oil
1/2 t. salt
1/8 t. pepper
1 eggplant, cut into 1/4-inch
slices

1 zucchini, cut into 8 slices
1 red pepper, quartered
8 slices ciabatta bread
1 c. shredded mozzarella cheese
8 fresh basil leaves

Whisk vinegar, oil, salt and pepper in a bowl; set aside. Spray a baking sheet with non-stick vegetable spray. Brush both sides of eggplant and zucchini with vinegar mixture. Arrange in a single layer on baking sheet. Coat all vegetables with vegetable spray. Broil 4 inches from heat for 7 to 8 minutes, turning once. Lightly brush one side of each bread slice with remaining vinegar mixture; coat other side with spray. Place bread, sprayed-side down, on an ungreased baking sheet. Top with vegetables, cheese, basil and remaining bread, sprayed-side up. Place sandwiches, one at a time, in a skillet; set a bacon press or other weight on top. Cook over medium-high heat for about 4 minutes per side, until lightly golden.

Whip up some herbed dill butter to use in fish sandwiches. Blend 2 tablespoons softened butter, 2 tablespoons lemon juice, a teaspoon of minced garlic and a teaspoon of fresh dill...heavenly!

Seaside Salmon Buns

Serves 6

14-oz. can salmon, drained and
    flaked
1/4 c. green pepper, chopped
1 T. onion, chopped
2 t. lemon juice

1-1/4 c. mayonnaise, divided
6 hamburger buns, split
12 thick tomato slices
1/2 c. shredded Cheddar cheese

Mix salmon, pepper, onion, lemon juice and 1/2 cup mayonnaise.
Pile salmon mixture onto bun halves; top each with a tomato slice.
Arrange buns on an ungreased baking sheet. Mix remaining
mayonnaise with cheese; spread over tomato slices. Broil until lightly
golden and cheese is melted.

Try using colorful flavored wraps and tortillas for
roll-ups...sun-dried tomato-basil, garlic-herb or cilantro
really give them a zippy new taste.

Crunchy Tuna Roll-Ups

Makes 8 servings

2 6-oz. cans tuna, drained
1/2 c. sliced water chestnuts,
    chopped
1/2 c. green onion, chopped
1/3 c. red pepper, chopped

Optional: 4 eggs, hard-boiled,
    peeled and chopped
1/2 c. mayonnaise
4 8-inch flour tortillas
2 c. romaine lettuce, shredded

Combine all ingredients except tortillas and lettuce; spread on tortillas.
Sprinkle with lettuce and roll up each tortilla tightly. Slice in half
diagonally; wrap in plastic wrap and refrigerate up to 3 hours
before serving.

Looking for a change from mayonnaise or mustard when making sandwich wraps? Give herbed spreadable cream cheese a try...yum!

Crabby Avocado Salad Wraps

Makes 4 servings

1 lb. crabmeat
3 T. mayonnaise
1 t. dry mustard
1/2 c. celery, chopped

salt and pepper to taste
2 avocados, pitted and sliced
4 10-inch flour tortillas

Combine crabmeat, mayonnaise, mustard, celery, salt and pepper; mix well. Top each tortilla with several avocado slices and a scoop of crabmeat mixture. Roll up.

Stir mandarin orange segments into sweet, creamy coleslaw for a yummy change of pace.

Asian Chicken Wraps

Makes 4 wraps

2 boneless, skinless chicken
    breasts, cooked and
    shredded
2/3 c. General Tso's sauce
1/4 c. teriyaki sauce
4 10-inch flour tortillas

10-oz. pkg. romaine and
    cabbage salad mix
1/2 c. carrot, peeled and
    shredded
4 T. sliced almonds
2 T. chow mein noodles

Combine chicken and sauces in a skillet. Warm over medium heat; set aside. Divide ingredients evenly on each tortilla, beginning with salad mix, carrots, chicken mixture, almonds and ending with chow mein noodles. Roll up burrito style.

Use a damp sponge sprinkled with baking soda to scrub fruits & veggies...it works just as well as expensive cleansers for vegetables.

Ranch BLT Wraps

Makes 6

6 leaves green leaf lettuce
6 sandwich wraps
12-oz. pkg. bacon, crisply
    cooked

1 lb. boneless, skinless chicken
    breasts, cooked and cubed
2 tomatoes, diced
ranch salad dressing to taste

Place one leaf lettuce on each sandwich wrap. Top with 2 to 3 slices bacon. Spoon chicken and tomatoes evenly over bacon. Drizzle with salad dressing and roll up.

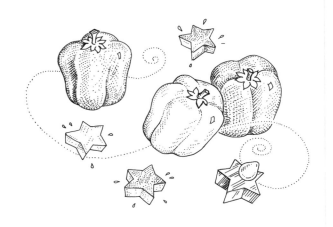

Brighten a dinner plate with edible fruit and veggie
garnishes...try carrot curls, red or yellow pepper stars,
radish roses, pineapple spears or kiwi slices.

Deli Skillet Sandwiches

Makes 4 sandwiches

8 slices rye bread
1/4 lb. cooked ham, thinly
   sliced
1/4 lb. provolone cheese, thinly
   sliced

1/4 lb. cooked turkey, thinly
   sliced
1/2 c. milk
2 eggs

On each of 4 slices of bread, layer ham, cheese and turkey. Top with remaining bread and press lightly to make 4 sandwiches. Cut each sandwich in 1/2 diagonally; set aside. In a 9" pie plate, beat together milk and eggs until well blended. Dip each sandwich into egg mixture, coating both sides. Cook, in a preheated greased skillet, over medium heat until golden, turning once. Transfer to a baking sheet. Bake at 400 degrees for 3 to 5 minutes, or until cheese melts and sandwiches are heated through.

There's nothing cozier than tomato soup and grilled cheese for supper! Just for fun, make grilled cheese sandwiches in a waffle iron.

Heavenly Hot Ham & Cheese

Serves 4

1 lb. very thinly sliced deli ham
1/2 lb. American cheese, diced
1/3 c. mayonnaise
1/3 c. brown mustard

1/3 c. sweet pickle relish
1 onion, finely chopped
4 hamburger buns, split

Combine all ingredients except buns; spoon onto buns. Wrap individually in aluminum foil; place on a baking sheet. Bake at 350 degrees for 20 minutes.

Handy gadgets like mini choppers make prep work a breeze for
chopping onions, tomatoes or peppers...what a timesaver!

Grilled Cuban Sandwiches

Makes 4 servings

1 loaf French bread, halved
  lengthwise
2 T. Dijon mustard
6-oz. pkg. Swiss cheese, thinly
  sliced

6-oz. pkg. deli ham, thinly
  sliced
6-oz. pkg. deli roast pork,
  thinly sliced
8 dill pickle sandwich slices

Spread cut sides of bread with mustard. Arrange half each of cheese, ham and pork on bottom half of bread; top with pickle slices. Repeat layering with remaining cheese and meat; cover with top half of bread. Slice into quarters. Arrange sandwiches in a skillet that has been sprayed with non-stick vegetable spray; place a heavy skillet on top of sandwiches. Cook over medium-high heat for 2 minutes on each side, or until golden and cheese is melted.

Spice up a favorite sandwich melt! Instead of
Cheddar or mozzarella cheese, try Mexican-blend or
Pepper Jack cheese. Zesty!

Grilled Salami Pizza Sandwiches

Makes 4

2/3 c. pizza sauce
8 slices bread
4 slices deli salami

4 slices American cheese
garlic salt to taste
1 T. butter, softened

Spread pizza sauce on one side of 4 bread slices. Top each bread slice with one salami slice and one cheese slice; sprinkle with garlic salt. Top with remaining bread slices. Generously butter top and bottom of sandwiches. Heat a skillet over medium heat; add sandwiches and cook on both sides until bread is toasted and cheese is melted.

Mini sandwiches are fun for parties...everyone can take just what they want! Use mini brown & serve rolls, bagels or pitas instead of full-size buns.

Pizzawiches

Serves 6 to 8

1 lb. ground beef
1 onion, diced
4-oz. jar sliced mushrooms,
    drained
16-oz. jar pizza sauce

6 to 8 slices mozzarella cheese
6 to 8 hamburger or sub buns,
    split
Optional: sliced olives,
    pepperoni slices

In a skillet over medium heat, brown ground beef and onion; drain.
Add mushrooms and pizza sauce to skillet; heat through. Assemble
sandwiches with ground beef mixture and cheese slices, adding olives
and pepperoni if desired.

Stem and seed a green pepper in a flash...hold the pepper upright on a cutting board. Use a sharp knife to slice each of the sides from the pepper. You'll then have four large seedless pieces that can easily be chopped!

Italian Sausage Sandwiches

Serves 4

4 t. butter, softened
4 hoagie rolls, split
garlic powder to taste
1 lb. Italian pork sausage links

1 green pepper, sliced
1 onion, sliced
8-oz. pkg. shredded mozzarella
   cheese

Spread one teaspoon butter on each roll and sprinkle with garlic powder; place on an ungreased baking sheet butter-side up. Bake at 350 degrees until lightly toasted; set aside. Brown sausages in a large skillet over medium heat until cooked through; remove from heat. Add green pepper and onion to skillet; cook until tender, 2 to 3 minutes. Arrange sausages in rolls; evenly top with green pepper, onion and cheese. Place on baking sheet; bake at 350 degrees until cheese is melted, about 5 minutes.

Bright bandannas make colorful table napkins...find them in shades
of blue, pink, yellow, red and green. Tie one around each set of
flatware for lap-size napkins, then, after lunch, toss them
in the washer...so easy!

Roast Beef & Pepper Panini   *Makes 4 sandwiches*

8 thick slices Italian bread
8 slices deli roast beef
4 slices mozzarella cheese
8-oz. jar roasted red peppers,
    drained and chopped

2 T. green olives with pimentos,
    diced
1 T. olive oil

Top 4 slices bread with roast beef, cheese, peppers and olives; add remaining bread slices. Brush oil lightly over both sides of sandwiches. Heat a large skillet over medium heat. Add sandwiches and cook for 2 to 3 minutes on each side, until golden and cheese has melted. Slice sandwiches in half to serve.

A pizza cutter is oh-so handy for slicing cheesy quesadillas into wedges...clever!

BLT Quesadilla

Makes one serving

1 t. butter
2 10-inch flour tortillas
1/3 c. shredded Cheddar Jack
    cheese
2 slices bacon, crisply cooked
    and crumbled

1/2 tomato, chopped
1 to 2 t. onion, chopped
fajita seasoning to taste

Melt butter in a skillet over medium heat; add one tortilla and cook until golden. While tortilla is still in skillet, sprinkle with cheese, bacon, tomato, onion and seasoning. Top with remaining tortilla; turn carefully and cook until golden and cheese has melted. Slice into quarters to serve.

The ambition of every good cook...to make something
very good with the fewest possible ingredients.

-Urbain Dubois

Yummy Chicken Quesadillas *Makes 4 to 6 servings*

2 yellow onions, sliced
4 T. olive oil, divided
8 to 12 6-inch corn tortillas
16-oz. pkg. shredded Monterey
    Jack cheese

3-lb. deli roast chicken,
    shredded or cubed
Optional: guacamole, salsa

In a large skillet over medium-high heat, sauté onions in 2 tablespoons oil until golden and caramelized. Add a drizzle of remaining oil to a separate skillet; cook a tortilla for 15 seconds on each side. Spoon onions, cheese and chicken onto half of tortilla; fold over and cook for about one minute, until light golden and crisp, or just until cheese melts for a soft quesadilla. Repeat with remaining ingredients; garnish as desired.

If there's leftover salad after dinner, use it for a tasty sandwich filling the next day. Split a pita round, stuff with salad, chopped chicken or turkey, sliced grapes and drizzle with salad dressing.

Steak & Blue Cheese Quesadilla Salad   *Serves 4*

1/2 lb. beef flank steak
1/4 t. salt
1/4 t. pepper
1/2 c. crumbled blue cheese
4 8-inch flour tortillas
1 head lettuce, torn

1 c. red onion, sliced
2 tomatoes, cut into 8 wedges
  each
Optional: 1 avocado, pitted,
  peeled and sliced
favorite salad dressing to taste

Sprinkle steak with salt and pepper. Grill steak over a medium-hot grill for about 4 minutes per side. Let stand for 5 minutes. Thinly slice steak diagonally across the grain; set aside. Sprinkle cheese evenly over 2 tortillas. Divide steak evenly over cheese; top with remaining tortillas. Heat a greased skillet over medium heat; cook quesadillas 4 minutes per side, or until golden. Cut each into 8 wedges. Combine vegetables in a bowl; drizzle with dressing and toss well. Divide salad among 4 plates; top each serving with 4 wedges.

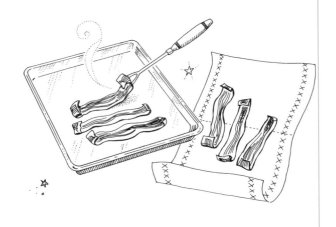

Crispy bacon makes any sandwich a winner! Lay slices on a jelly-roll pan and bake at 350 degrees for 15 to 20 minutes, until they're as crisp as you like. Drain well on paper towels.

Philly Cheesesteak Sandwiches

Makes 6

2 T. butter
1 lb. beef top sirloin or ribeye
    steak, thinly sliced
seasoned salt and pepper to
    taste
1 onion, chopped

1 clove garlic, chopped
Optional: 1 c. sliced mushrooms
1 green pepper, chopped
1 lb. provolone, Gouda or Swiss
    cheese, sliced
6 hoagie buns or baguettes, split

Melt butter in a skillet over medium heat. Add steak; sprinkle with
seasoned salt and pepper and sauté just until browned. Add onion,
garlic, mushrooms, if using, and green pepper; stir. Cover and simmer
for 5 to 7 minutes, until onion and pepper have softened slightly.
Add additional salt and pepper to taste. Remove from heat; set aside.
Lay 2 to 3 slices cheese in each bun; top with 2 to 3 tablespoonfuls
of steak mixture. Top with additional cheese, if desired. Wrap each
sandwich in aluminum foil; bake at 350 degrees for 10 to
15 minutes, until cheese is melted.

Toast sandwich buns before adding shredded or sliced meat...it only takes a minute and makes such a tasty difference. Buns will drip less too...less mess!

Grilled Roast Beef Sandwiches

Serves 5

4-1/2 oz. can chopped green
    chiles, drained
2 T. mayonnaise
1 T. Dijon mustard

10 slices rye bread
5 slices Swiss cheese
10 slices deli roast beef
1/4 c. butter, softened

Combine chiles, mayonnaise and mustard together; spread about one tablespoon mixture on 5 slices of bread. Top each with one slice cheese, 2 slices roast beef and remaining bread slices. Spread butter on outsides of sandwiches; place on a broiler pan or on the grill. Broil or grill each side until golden.

Whip up a zippy Tex-Mex side dish pronto! Prepare instant rice, using chicken broth instead of water. Stir in a generous dollop of spicy salsa, top with shredded cheese and cover until cheese melts.

Texas Steak Sandwiches

Makes 4 sandwiches

8 slices frozen Texas toast
1 lb. deli roast beef, sliced
steak sauce to taste

8 slices provolone cheese
Optional: sliced green pepper
and red onion, sautéed

Bake Texas toast at 425 degrees for about 5 minutes per side, until softened and lightly golden; set aside. Warm roast beef in a skillet over medium heat until most of juices have evaporated; stir in steak sauce. Divide beef evenly among 4 toast slices; top with cheese slices, pepper and onion, if desired. Place beef-topped toast and remaining toast on a baking sheet; bake at 425 degrees until cheese is melted. Combine to form sandwiches.

To grate or shred a block of cheese easily, place the
wrapped cheese in the freezer for 10 to 20 minutes...
it will just glide across the grater!

Sausage-Spinach Pitas

Makes 12

1 lb. ground Italian pork
    sausage
10-oz. pkg. frozen chopped
    spinach

2 c. shredded mozzarella cheese
1/8 t. nutmeg
12 mini pita rounds

In a large skillet over medium heat, brown sausage. Add spinach
and cook until spinach is thawed; drain. Add cheese and nutmeg;
toss. Spoon into pita rounds and place them on an ungreased baking
sheet. Bake at 350 degrees for 20 minutes, or until hot.

Cool Yogurt Sauce is delicious in wraps. Use a fork to mash together a minced garlic clove, 3 tablespoons chopped walnuts and one teaspoon olive oil. Stir into a 16-ounce container of plain yogurt. Add salt & pepper to taste and chill.

Mediterranean Chicken Wraps

4 roma tomatoes, peeled and
   sliced
1/2 c. crumbled feta cheese
2 T. lemon juice
1/4 c. olive oil
salt and pepper to taste

4 boneless, skinless chicken
   breasts, grilled and sliced
4 whole-wheat flat breads
Garnish: Yogurt Sauce (opposite
   page), lettuce, Kalamata
   olives, sliced red onion

Combine tomatoes, cheese, lemon juice and oil. Sprinkle with salt and
pepper. Fold in chicken; arrange in flat breads. Top with Yogurt Sauce;
garnish with lettuce, olives and onion.

A healthy light wrap for smaller appetites...place sandwich toppings on lettuce leaves instead of bread and roll up.

Ranch Chicken Wraps

Makes 8 to 10 wraps

4 boneless, skinless chicken
   breasts, sliced into strips
1 T. oil
2.8-oz. can French fried onions
1/4 c. bacon bits

8-oz. pkg. shredded Cheddar
   cheese
lettuce leaves
8 to 10 8-inch flour tortillas
Garnish: ranch salad dressing

In a large non-stick skillet over medium heat, cook chicken in oil until golden and juices run clear. Add onions, bacon bits and cheese to skillet; cook until cheese melts. Place several lettuce leaves on each tortilla and spoon chicken mixture on top. Top with salad dressing and roll up.

When you're making quesadillas for a crowd, keep them warm
in a low-temperature oven. Just arrange quesadillas on
a baking sheet, set in the oven, then serve as needed.

Green Chile-Chicken Quesadillas *Makes 8 servings*

1 lb. boneless, skinless chicken
   breasts, cubed
3 T. oil, divided
15-oz. can black beans, drained
   and rinsed
8-3/4 oz. can corn, drained
4-oz. can diced green chiles

1-1/4 oz. pkg. white chicken
   chili seasoning mix
1/4 c. water
8 8-inch flour tortillas
8-oz. pkg. shredded
   Mexican-blend cheese

Over medium-high heat, sauté chicken in one tablespoon oil until golden. Add vegetables, seasoning mix and water; reduce heat and simmer for 6 to 8 minutes. Spoon 1/2 cup chicken mixture and 1/4 cup cheese onto each tortilla; fold in half, pressing down lightly. Brush outsides of tortillas lightly with remaining oil. Grill over medium heat for 2 to 3 minutes on each side, turning carefully, until golden and cheese melts. Cut into wedges to serve.

Sun-warmed ripe tomatoes from the farmers' market...is there anything more irresistible? Serve them simply, drizzled with a little Italian salad dressing and some chopped fresh basil.

Sweet Onion Quesadillas

Makes 3 to 6 servings

1 to 2 sweet onions, sliced
1 T. butter
6 8-inch flour tortillas, divided
8-oz. pkg. shredded Mexican-
blend cheese
Garnish: sour cream

Sauté onions in butter over medium heat until tender and golden.
Spoon onto 3 tortillas; sprinkle with cheese. Top with remaining
tortillas. Place quesadillas on a medium-hot grill; cook until lightly
golden on bottom. Turn over carefully; cook until golden on other
side. Remove from grill and cut into wedges. Serve with sour cream.

Serve up a festive sandwich buffet for an oh-so-easy gathering.
Set out a savory selection of deli meats, cheeses, breads and
other fixin's for make-your-own-sandwiches...even gourmet
mustards. Add a tabletop grill for making hot sandwiches,
then just relax and enjoy your guests.

Bacon Quesadillas

Makes 4 servings

1 c. shredded Colby Jack cheese
1/4 c. bacon bits
1/4 c. green onion, thinly sliced
Optional: 4-oz. can green chiles

Optional: 1/4 c. red or green
   pepper, chopped
4 6-inch flour tortillas
Garnish: sour cream, salsa

Combine cheese, bacon bits and onion in a small bowl; add chiles and peppers, if desired. Sprinkle mixture equally over each tortilla. Fold tortillas in half; press lightly to seal edges. Arrange on a lightly greased baking sheet. Bake at 400 degrees for 8 to 10 minutes, until edges are lightly golden. Top with a dollop of sour cream and salsa.

Search out yard sales or auctions for vintage tablecloths and tea towels with brightly colored fruit motifs...they'll add a dash of fun to any sandwich supper.

Chili Dog Wraps

Makes 10 servings

10 6 or 8-inch flour or corn
    tortillas
10 hot dogs
16-oz. can chili

16-oz. jar salsa
1 c. shredded Cheddar or
    Monterey Jack cheese

Warm tortillas as directed on package. Place one hot dog and
3 tablespoons chili on each tortilla. Roll up tortillas; place seam-side
down in a greased 13"x9" baking pan. Spoon salsa over tortillas.
Cover and bake at 350 degrees for 20 minutes. Sprinkle with
cheese and bake, uncovered, about 5 minutes longer, or until
cheese has melted.

Make some tangy pickled veggies next time you finish a jar of dill pickles! Simply cut up fresh carrots, green peppers, celery and other vegetables, drop them into the leftover pickle juice and refrigerate for a few days.

Gooey Buns

Makes 24 sandwiches

1 lb. deli bologna, cubed
3/4 lb. pasteurized process
    cheese spread, cubed
1/3 c. mayonnaise-type salad
    dressing

1/4 c. mustard
1/4 c. dried, minced onion
sweet pickle relish to taste
24 hot dog buns, split

Grind bologna and cheese together in a food processor. Add remaining ingredients except buns; mix thoroughly. Spread generously in buns; wrap tightly in aluminum foil. Arrange on a baking sheet. Bake at 325 degrees for 25 minutes.

Instead of one large picnic basket, why not pack individual lunches for everyone in children's sand pails? Line the pails with checked napkins and tie a name tag to the handle of each pail.

Picnic Pinwheels

1/3 c. creamy peanut butter
4 8-inch flour tortillas

1 c. banana, chopped
1/4 c. low-fat granola cereal

Spread peanut butter on each tortilla; top with banana and granola.
Tightly roll up tortillas and cut each one in half. Wrap roll-ups in
plastic wrap or aluminum foil to pack in lunchboxes.

When butter is too cold to spread, turn a hot bowl over the butter dish. It will soften, but not melt.

Grilled PB&J

8 slices bread
4 T. creamy peanut butter
4 T. grape jelly or strawberry
    jam

1/4 c. milk
1 egg, beaten
1 T. vanilla extract
1 t. cinnamon

Spread 4 slices of bread with peanut butter and jelly or jam; top with remaining bread. Whisk together remaining ingredients in a shallow bowl. Brush milk mixture on one side of sandwiches. Place moistened side down in a lightly greased skillet; brush milk mixture over top. Grill until golden on both sides.

Fruit kabobs are a sweet ending to any meal. Arrange chunks of
pineapple and banana, plump strawberries and orange wedges
on skewers. For a creamy dipping sauce, blend together
1/2 cup each of cream cheese and marshmallow creme.

Chocolate Quesadillas

Serves 6

6 8-inch flour tortillas
2 T. butter, melted

1 c. milk chocolate chips
Garnish: vanilla ice cream

Brush both sides of each tortilla with melted butter; arrange in a single layer on an ungreased baking sheet. Sprinkle chocolate chips on half of each tortilla; fold over tortillas. Bake for 4 to 6 minutes at 450 degrees until golden. Top each with a scoop of vanilla ice cream.

INDEX

INDEX

Our Story

Back in 1984, we were next-door neighbors raising our families in the little town of Delaware, Ohio. Two moms with small children, we were looking for a way to do what we loved and stay home with the kids too. We had always shared a love of home cooking and making memories with family & friends and so, after many a conversation over the backyard fence, **Gooseberry Patch** was born.

We put together our first catalog at our kitchen tables, enlisting the help of our loved ones wherever we could. From that very first mailing, we found an immediate connection with many of our customers and it wasn't long before we began receiving letters, photos and recipes from these new friends. In 1992, we put together our very first cookbook, compiled from hundreds of these recipes and, the rest, as they say, is history.

Hard to believe it's been over 25 years since those kitchen-table days! From that original little **Gooseberry Patch** family, we've grown to include an amazing group of creative folks who love cooking, decorating and creating as much as we do. Today, we're best known for our homestyle, family-friendly cookbooks, now recognized as national bestsellers.

One thing's for sure, we couldn't have done it without our friends all across the country. Each year, we're honored to turn thousands of your recipes into our collectible cookbooks. Our hope is that each book captures the stories and heart of all of you who have shared with us. Whether you've been with us since the beginning or are just discovering us, welcome to the **Gooseberry Patch** family!

Vickie & JoAnn

Want to hear the latest from **Gooseberry Patch**?
www.gooseberrypatch.com

Join Our Circle of Friends

You Tube

Read Our Blog

Find us on Facebook

Follow us on twitter

1•800•854•6673